This book belongs to…

_____

NEW Cultural Screen Time!
Cultural Videos, Animations & Rhymes with Maya, Neel & Chintu!

SUBSCRIBE TO OUR CHANNEL

CultureGroove.com/youtube

Pronunciation Guide

Chhoti – Chh-o-tee

Chintu – Chin-too

Gujia – Goo-jee-yaa

Gulaal – Goo-laal

Holi – Ho-lee

Holika – Ho-lee-kaa

Pichkari – Pitch-kaa-ree

Prahlad – Pruh-laad

Thandai – Thun-da-yee

Note for parents: Our books provide a glimpse into the beautiful cultural diversity of India, including occasional mythology references. Given India's size and diversity, Holi is celebrated in a multitude of different ways. In this book, we showcase elements of Holi that are best suited for young readers to follow.

Copyright © 2016, 2017, 2018, 2019, 2020 by Bollywood Groove™, Culture Groove. All rights reserved. This book or any portion thereof may not be reproduced or used in any manner whatsoever without the express written permission of the publisher except for the use of brief quotations in a book review.
Printed in the United States of America. First Edition.

Maya & Neel's India Adventure Series, Book 14

Holi
50 ACTIVITY BOOK
Holi Dance Choreographies, Storytime, Craft, Recipes, Puzzles, Word games, Coloring & More!

Written by:
Ajanta & Vivek

Raise Multicultural Kids

Welcome to Culture Groove!

Dear Parents, Educators & Young Readers,

Thank you for exploring Culture Groove's **Holi** Activity Book! We've created a one-stop kit for all your Holi teaching and celebration needs.

From story time, Holi dance choreographies and recipes to puzzles, word games, craft and coloring activities, this book has it all.

Our mission, quite simply, is to help **Raise Multicultural Kids**. Whether it's through our classes, digital resources or books, we work tirelessly to help kids everywhere see the world with a multicultural lens. This lens, in turn, helps them develop understanding, empathy, and curiosity about the world.

As parents of a young kid who is growing up outside of India, we are also very aware of the need to help better **connect kids to their roots**. We hope our work helps you as well.

Lastly, our content is not religious. It is specially focused on highlighting the cultural aspects of this beautiful festival.

Wishing you a very Happy Holi from our family to yours!

Ajanta, Vivek & Ruhaan

50 Holi Activities

1. Meet your Friends
2. Read the Holi Book
3. It's Storytime
4. Find the missing letters
5. Sliding Pichkari Card
6. Color your Holi friends
7. Scarf Friendship Game
8. Prahlad's Mytho Maze
9. Neel's Holi Crossword
10. Holi Dance 1 - Ja Re Hat
11. Holi Riddles
12. Thandai Recipe
13. Holi Dance 2 – Dancing Bookworms
14. I am Brave When…
15. Lotus Flower Craft
16. Color by number
17. Indoor / Classroom Plan
18. Holi Flash Cards
19. Learn Holi words
20. Holi Dance 3 - Holiya Main
21. Find all Holi items
22. Maya's Word Search
23. Holi Dance 4 - Holi Shark
24. Holi Spot & Color
25. Help Chintu on Friendship Ladder
26. Holi Pasta Bracelets
27. Draw the other half
28. Magic Messages
29. Indian Flower fun facts
30. Count the Indian Flowers
31. Healthy Gujia Recipe
32. Fill the boxes
33. Holi Dance 5 - Madhubala
34. Celebration Tracker
35. Holi Dance 6 – Hindi Finger Family
36. Match the Hindi Colors
37. Yummy moon phases
38. Spot the 8 differences
39. Holi Double puzzle
40. Holi Dance 7 - Jai Jai Shiv Shankar
41. How many Pichkaris can you find
42. Make Holi colors
43. Holi Secret Message
44. Who likes which flower?
45. Connect the dots
46. Hindi Color Hop
47. My Holi journal
48. Holi Jigsaw Puzzle
49. Prahlad Bonfire Craft
50. Moon countdown

What is Holi all about?

Being Brave

As you will learn in story time, a brave little boy named Prahlad wins over an evil king.

That is why we celebrate the victory of good over evil. In this book, we will do a few activities about being brave!

Spring

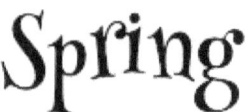

Holi is a spring festival. This is when trees have new green leaves and flowers are blooming. We will do some fun Spring-themed activities.

Holi Colors

And of course, Holi is all about playing with colors! Get ready for some fun color-themed activities.

Friendship

One of the most important messages of Holi is that of friendship.

Everyone is your friend on the day of Holi. And we play Holi by saying "Holi Hai"! Get ready to do some fun activities related to friendship.

Holi food

Holi is also a time for eating and drinking yummy food and drinks! We will try out some easy Holi recipes.

Dances

Holi isn't complete without a fun dance party! Get ready to learn some cool moves.

1. Meet your Friends

Meet Maya, the girl who goes on an adventure to India to celebrate Holi!

Meet Neel, the boy who goes on an adventure to India to celebrate Holi!

Meet Chintu, the pet squirrel, who joins Maya & Neel on all their adventures!

And together... they celebrate Holi!

2. Read the Holi Book
(BEST-SELLER)

Hey Kids!

Ready to experience Holi? It's the festival of colors and one of the most fun days in India.

Go on an adventure with Maya, Neel and their cute little partner, Chintu the squirrel!

You will learn about the story behind Holi, the colorful Holi markets, the incredible joy of playing Holi, the delicious Holi food & drinks and even about some unique ways of celebrating throughout the country.

This colorful and vibrant book will keep you engaged and learning for hours!

GET ON AMAZON WORLDWIDE:
CultureGroove.com/books

3. It's Storytime!

Join Maya, Neel and Chintu on their Holi adventure with this Read-Aloud video of our bestselling book "Let's Celebrate Holi!".

FIND IT ON OUR CULTURE CHANNEL
CultureGroove.com/Holi

4. Find the missing letters

Once, there was an evil __ing.

 Who wanted everyone to be __cared of him.

Prahlad was a little __oy, who was not afraid.

 The King's sister, Holika, had a __agical power.

She could not get hurt by __ire.

The King made Holika and Prahlad __it in the fire

But nothing happened to Prahlad. Instead Holika __isappeared!

Answers at the end

5. Sliding Pichkari Card

A Pichkari is what you use to splash colored water on each other. Make this Pichkari card that says "Holi Hai" in a fun & colorful way!

Note: All shape templates used in this craft are available for download & print at CultureGroove.com/Holi

Materials: cardstock, colors (crayons or paint), popsicle stick – optional.

Steps:

☐ Cut this shape below. We will call this the Pichkari base. Stick the base on a cardstock.

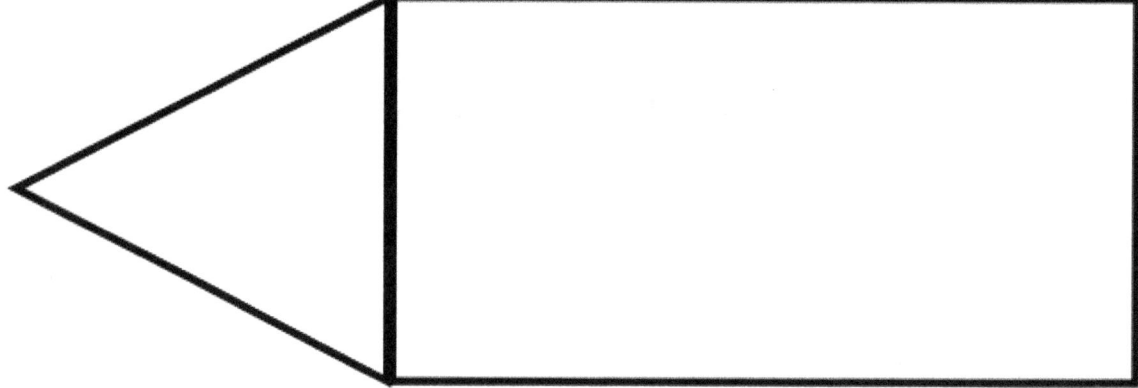

☐ Cut the shape below. We will call this the window. Make sure it is see-through.

- [ ] Apply glue on three sides of the window but not on the right short side

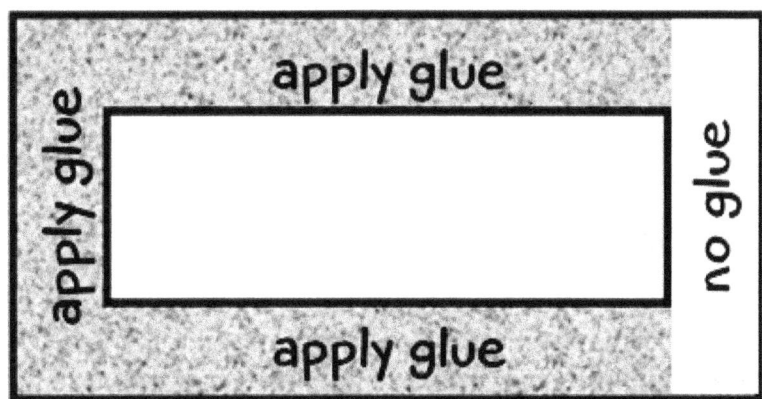

- [ ] Stick the "window" on top of the Pichkari base.

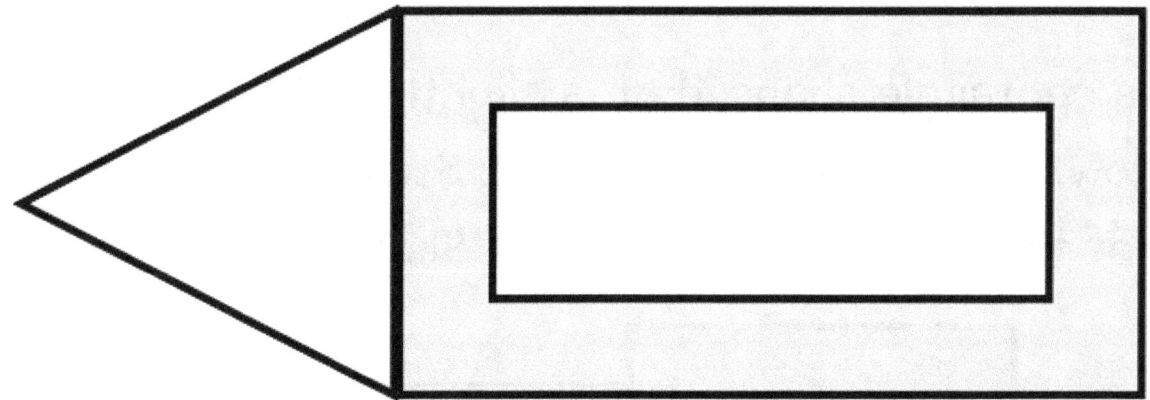

- [ ] With colorful markers or crayons, write "Holi Hai!" along with any other message in the area visible through the window.

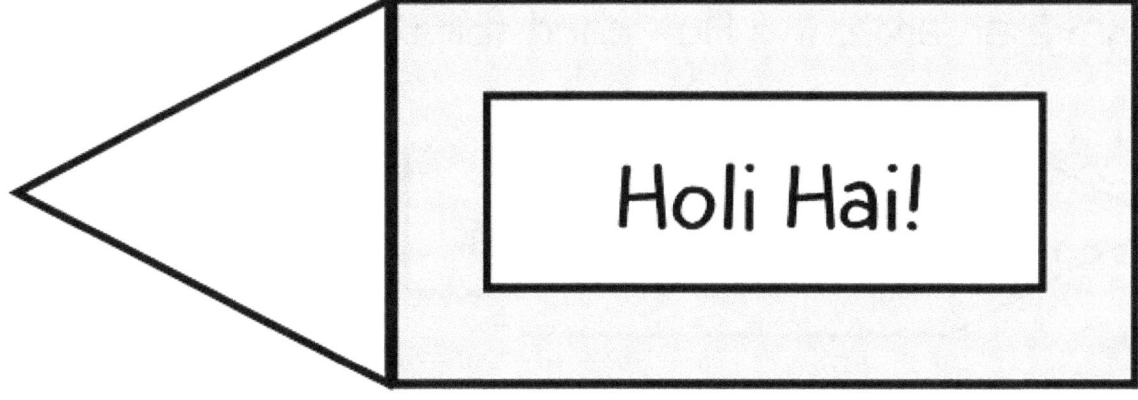

Pichkari Card Contd.

- ❏ For the slider, take a popsicle stick or cut out a rectangle in card stock. Also cut out a circle shape from cardstock. Stick the circle at the end of the stick.

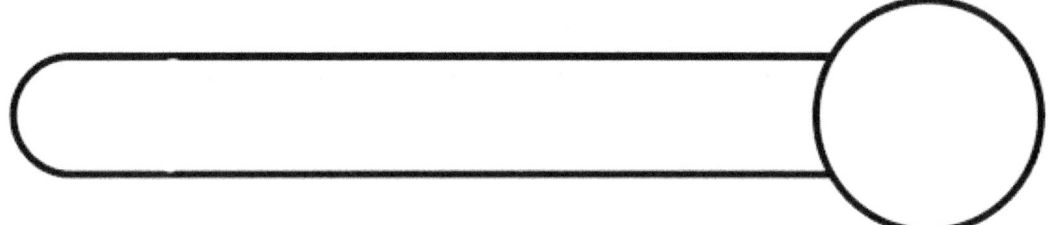

- ❏ Cut a rectangle shape that is slightly wider than the window opening of Pichkari base. Stick it to the other end of the popsicle stick. Write "Slide Me!" on it.

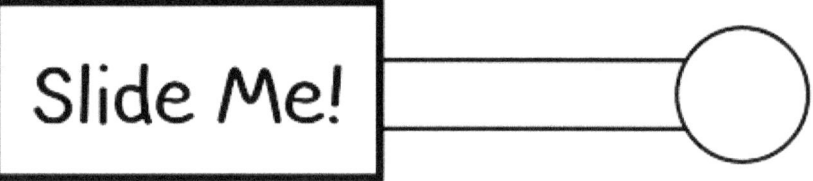

- ❏ Now you can slide the slider in and out of the Pichkari base. Color everything with fun & bright colors and you have an amazing Holi card for the festival!

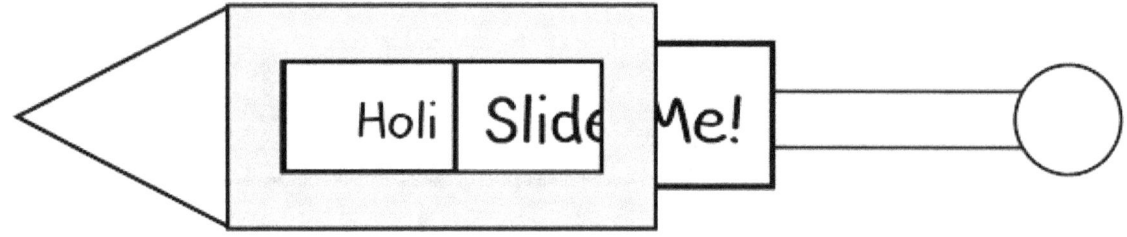

6. Color your Holi Friends

Everyone is your friend on Holi!
Throw colors and play Holi with all.

7. Scarf Friendship Game

This is a great icebreaker or classroom game

What you need
- [ ] Colorful scarves or small fabric pieces that kids can throw at each other
- [ ] Something to mark spots on the floor

Before you start
- [ ] Mark spots on the floor as shown above. Notice how kids will end up standing in pairs.
- [ ] Give one colorful scarf or fabric to each kid.
- [ ] Play some fun Holi music in the background.

How to play
- [ ] Begin with all the kids standing in one line.
- [ ] The first kid goes to spot #1 and:
    - [ ] Announces their name

- ❏ Their favorite Holi color
- ❏ Optionally does a fun dance move
- ❏ When the next kid goes to spot #2, they repeat all of these and then both of them throw their colorful scarf at each other and say "Holi Hai!"
- ❏ Next kid goes to spot #3, announces their details and then waits for their partner to join them.
- ❏ Once a kid goes to spot #4, the kids at spot #3 & #4 throw their scarves at each other while saying "Holi Hai!". Continue for the remaining kids.
- ❏ Once they are all on their spots, have them sit down and learn the name of their partner and their favorite color and write it on the friendship note below.

Today, I made a new friend while playing the Holi Scarf game!

My friend's name is _____

My friend's favorite Holi color is:

_____

8. Prahlad's Mytho Maze

Help brave Prahlad get to Holika and make her disappear!

9. Neel's Holi Crossword

Across
2. Nom nom snack
3. Fire couldn't hurt her
4. Can you say 'splash!'?
7. Yumm so refreshing
9. Everyone's your ___ on Holi

Down
1. Festival of colors
2. Rub it on
4. The brave boy
5. Chitter! chitter!
6. Girl adventurer
8. Boy adventurer

Answers at the end

10. Holi Dance 1 - Ja Re Hat

An old classic, remade for the new times. This song has a playful banter of two people playing Holi. This choreography is especially suited for ages 3 to 6 years.

FIND IT ON OUR CULTURE CHANNEL
CultureGroove.com/Holi

11. Holi Riddles

Turns your face to many shades of color
So much fun to rub on this powder

What is it?

Shaped like half a moon and oh so yummy
This crunchy snack, makes me happy in my tummy

What is it?

Dip it in a bucket, fill it up
There it goes, splish splash glub

What is it?

Wasn't scared of bad, this little brave boy
Won over evil, filling us with joy

Who is it?

Answers at the end

12. Thandai Recipe

Thandai is a refreshing Holi drink resembling a milkshake. Follow this simple recipe to make your own Thandai.

Ingredients
4 cups Milk, boiled and cooled
¼ cup sugar
1 pinch black pepper (optional)
¼ cup almonds
2 tbsp fennel seeds
½ tsp cardamom powder
Few Saffron strands (optional)

Let's do it!
1. Blend the almonds, fennel seeds and cardamom into a powder
2. Combine powder & milk in a deep bowl
3. Whisk and refrigerate for 2 hours
4. Strain the mixture through a strainer.
5. Add sugar, pepper powder & saffron
6. Mix well
7. Serve chilled

13. Holi Dance 2 – Dancing Bookworms

You have always listened to stories but how about something new? Let's do a dance that acts out the Holi story using fun moves!

FIND IT ON OUR CULTURE CHANNEL
CultureGroove.com/Holi

14. I am Brave when...

It took a lot of courage for Prahlad to stand up to the evil King. But each one of us is brave in our own way.

Which of these actions does a BRAVE person do?

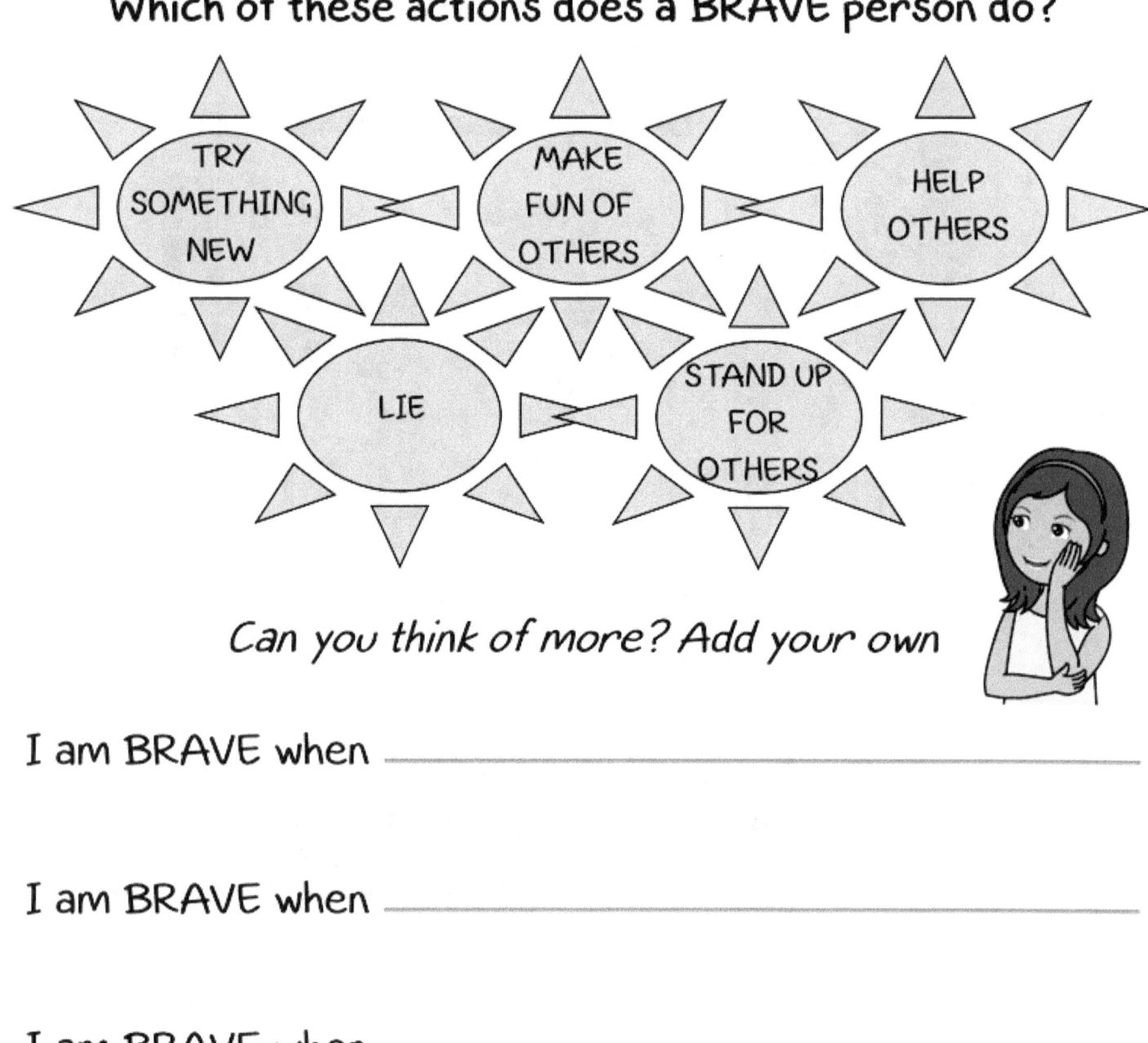

- TRY SOMETHING NEW
- MAKE FUN OF OTHERS
- HELP OTHERS
- LIE
- STAND UP FOR OTHERS

Can you think of more? Add your own

I am BRAVE when _____

I am BRAVE when _____

I am BRAVE when _____

15. Lotus Flower craft

Let's make a beautiful Lotus flower, the most important flower of India

Materials:
Pink colored paper, green colored paper, scissors, glue

Steps:
- ☐ First, cut a circle from green paper. Fold it in half and then fold again. Cut tiny triangles to give it a jagged edge.

- ☐ Next, cut petal shapes from pink colored paper. Cut a slit at the bottom. Bring the 2 edges together to give it a shape as shown. You can either glue or staple them together.

- ☐ Finally, stick the pink petals on the green leaf and your lotus flower is ready!

16. Color by Number

Color Chintu and his surroundings
according to the numbers below

1 Blue   4 Yellow
2 Orange   5 Red
3 Green   6 Brown

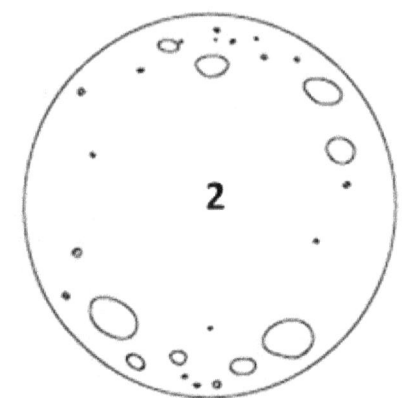

17. Indoor/Classroom Plan

Looking to bring the fun of Holi indoors or in a classroom? Try these 4 easy ideas.

If permitted, ask kids to wear their brightest clothes to school that day. The more colors, the better!

1. Time to Read!
- ☐ Start by reading "Let's Celebrate Holi!" book so kids learn all about the festival.

2. Time to Dance!
- ☐ Holi Shark is a fun one for very little kids.
- ☐ For kids ages 2 to 5, dance to "Ja re hat" and "Madhubala".
- ☐ For kids ages 7 to 10, dance to Holiya.
- ☐ For kids older than 10, try Jai Jai Shivshankar.

3. Time to Create!
- ☐ Pick from any of the craft or coloring activities and let the kids get creative.

4. Time to Play Holi!
- ☐ Put on our kid-friendly Holi playlist by visiting CultureGroove.com/Holi.
- ☐ On your cue, the kids can throw colored fabric/scarves, gently balled up colored tissue paper etc. up in the air and at each other.

18. Holi Flashcards

To download and make colored Holi flash cards,
Visit: CultureGroove.com/Holi

19. Learn Holi Words

Gulaal  Holi colored powder

Pichkari 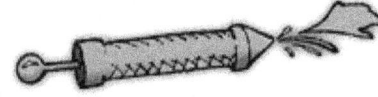 Holi water gun

Gujia 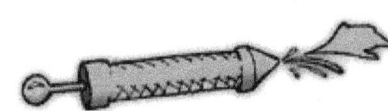 A sweet crunchy Holi snack

Thandai 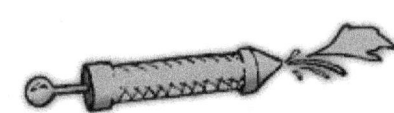 Milkshake-like Holi drink

Chaand 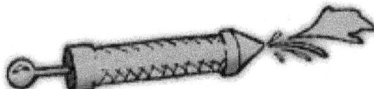 Moon

Basant  Spring

20. Holi Dance 3 - Holiya Main

A folk song from the state of Rajasthan, this song has some beautiful rhythms to match the colorful and vibrant culture of Rajasthan. This choreography is best suited for ages 7 to 10.

FIND IT ON OUR CULTURE CHANNEL
CultureGroove.com/Holi

21. Find all Holi Items

Can you find all the items related to Holi?
Think of not just colors but also food, sky, season etc.

Answers at the end

22. Maya's Word Search

```
A I M M H N O O M N
I X A O A Z J P U E
J L L D E Y I Q T E
U I E V N C A Y N L
G D A L H A R P I F
M R R K K Z H D H R
B K A I P L G T C I
R R L G N I R P S E
I O D A N C E Z Q N
H S K G U L A A L D
```

HELP MAYA FIND THESE WORDS

BRAVE	CHINTU	DANCE
FRIEND	GUJIA	GULAAL
HOLI	HOLIKA	MAYA
MOON	NEEL	PICHKARI
PRAHLAD	SPRING	THANDAI

Answers at the end

23. Holi Dance 4 - Holi Shark

Did you know? Baby shark loves to play Holi too. Learn this fun dance!

It's Holi do do do, it's Holi do do do, Holi Hai!

Throw some colors do do do, throw colors do do do, Holi Hai!

Splash some water do do do, splash water do do do, Holi Hai!

Eat Gujia do do do, eat Gujia do do do, Holi Hai!

Drink Thandai do do do, drink Thandai, Holi Hai!

Splash splash splash do do do,
Rub rub rub do do do,
Splash splash splash do do do,
Holi Hai!

Scrub scrub scrub do do do,
Clean clean clean do do do,
Holi is done, do do do,
So much fun!

FIND IT ON OUR CULTURE CHANNEL
CultureGroove.com/Holi

24. Holi Spot & Color

Complete the following sentences as you spot and color the objects on the next page:

On a _____ Moon Day,

in the _____ season,

we play Holi by splashing water with our _____

and putting _____ on each other.

We then eat some _____

and drink some _____.

Answers at the end

Holi Spot & Color contd.

25. Help Chintu climb the Friendship Ladder

Holi is a day when everyone is our friend. But we can be a good friend, all year long. Let's help Chintu be a good friend!

To play, start from the bottom and help Chintu with the answers. If you get it right, he moves up a step.

Chintu wins when he reaches the top of the ladder!

- Thank you for helping me be a good friend!
- Should I make fun of them?
- Should I ask before I take their things?
- Should I listen to their problems?
- Should I tell their secret to all other friends?
- Should I share with my friend?
- Should I help my friend?

26. Holi Pasta Bracelets

Let's make friendship pasta bracelets to give our friends!

Materials:
Any tube-shaped pasta, food coloring, rubbing alcohol, marker, plastic sealable bag

Steps:
- ❏ Cut the pasta into small pieces but big enough to write letters on them.
- ❏ Put them in a sealable plastic bag along with food coloring and rubbing alcohol and shake the bag. Repeat for multiple colors.
- ❏ Dry the pasta pieces. On each piece, using a marker, write a letter of a word that describes your friend, such as kind, strong, love, brave, helping, courage, sharing etc.
- ❏ String the pieces to make a bracelet. Gift the bracelets to your friends and show them how much they mean to you.

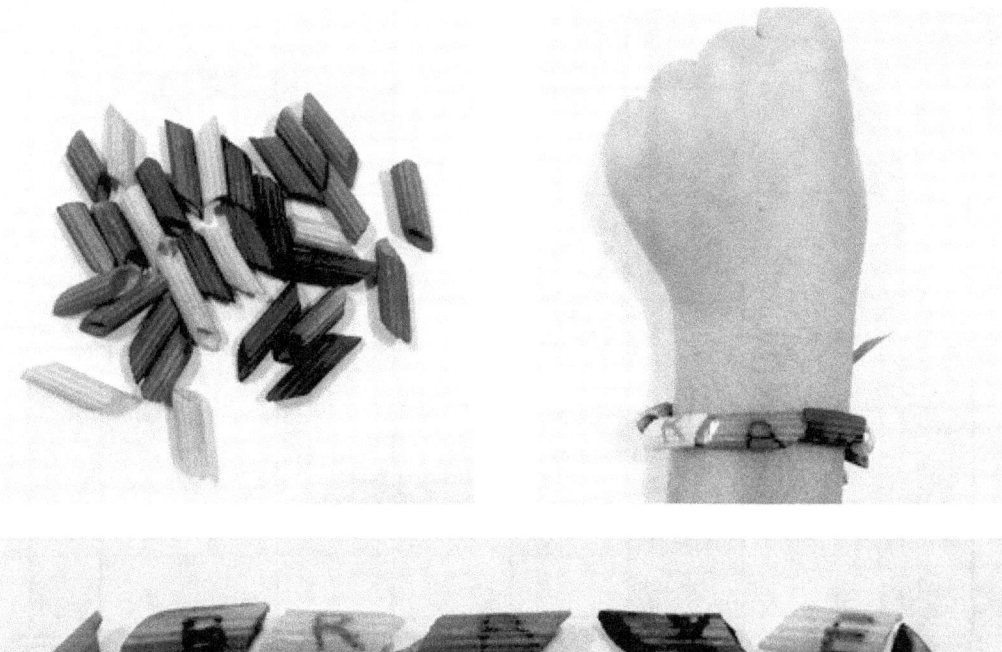

27. Draw the other half

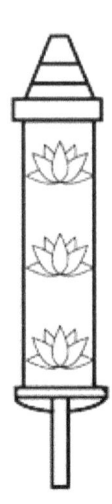
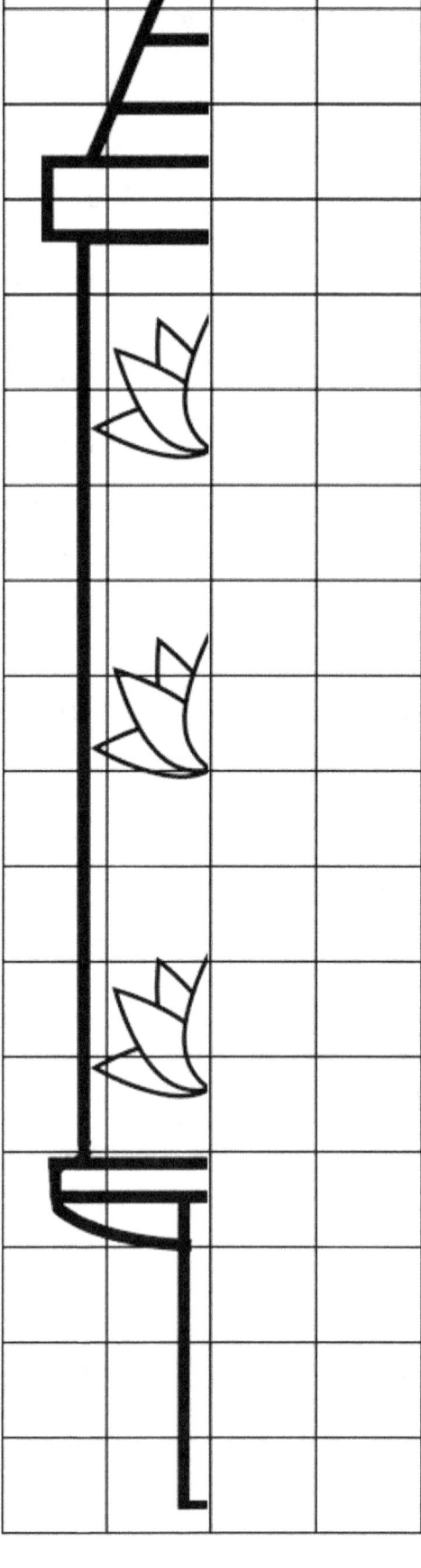
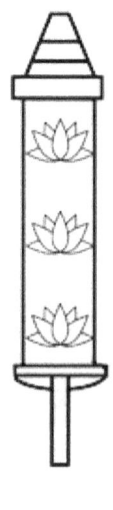

28. Magic Messages

The day before Holi is called Chhoti Holi (or mini-Holi) and is celebrated with a bonfire. The fire represents the victory of good over evil. Here is fun way to explore this concept.

Materials: paper, lemon juice, paint brush, candle

Let's do it!
- ☐ On a piece of paper, draw a check mark at the top and a cross at the bottom.
- ☐ Dip paint brush in lemon juice and write a word that represents something positive next to the checkmark. Let it dry.
- ☐ Make several more message like these.
- ☐ Now dip paint brush in water and write a word that represents something negative next to the cross.
- ☐ Hold the paper over a candle. Watch as the negative word disappears and the positive word slowly appears!

29. Indian Flower Fun Facts

Holi is a Spring festival when flowers are in full bloom.

Learn some fun facts about popular Indian flowers at CultureGroove.com/Holi

30. Count the Indian flowers

Circle the correct number of Indian Flowers

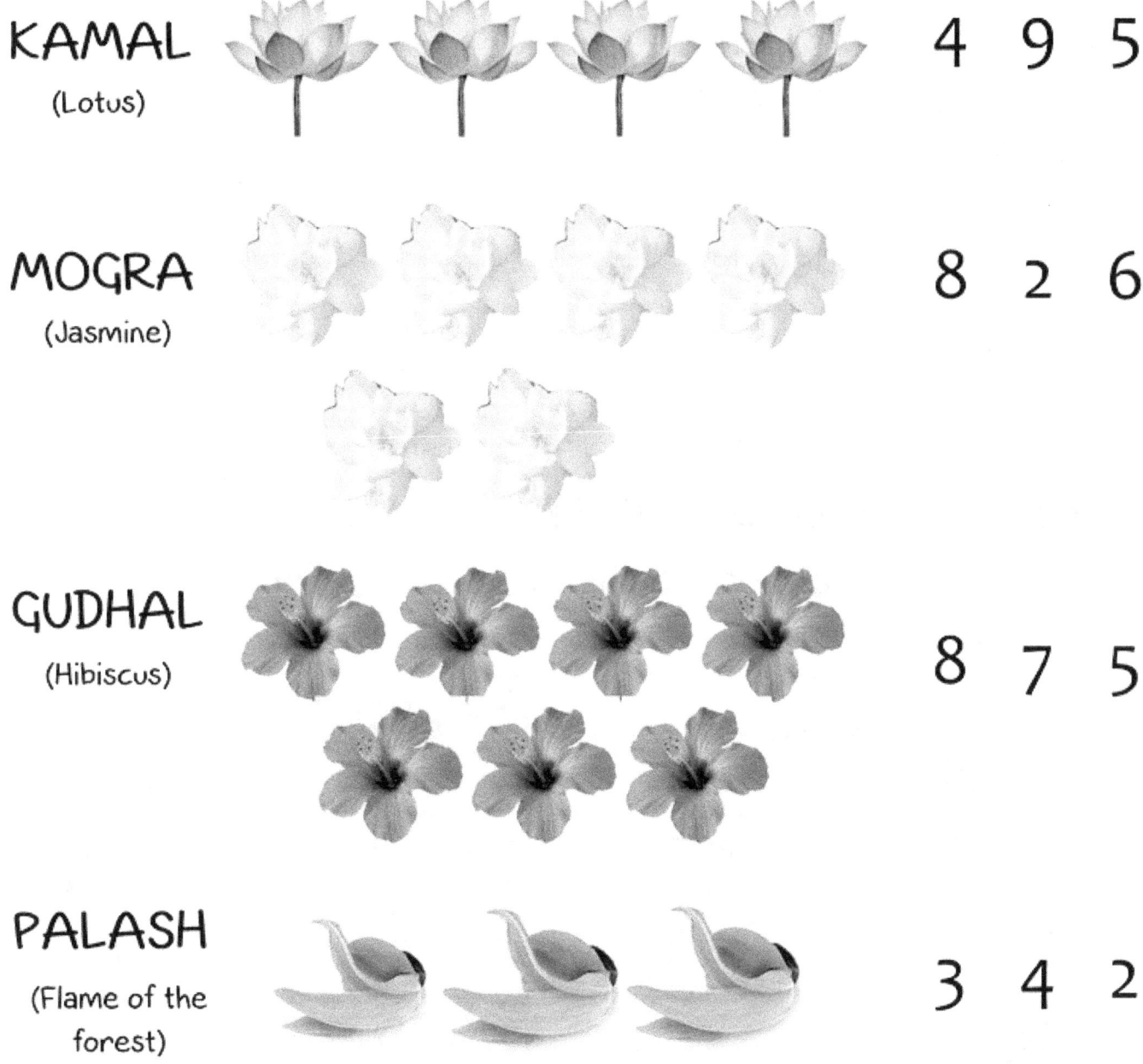

KAMAL (Lotus)   4   9   5

MOGRA (Jasmine)   8   2   6

GUDHAL (Hibiscus)   8   7   5

PALASH (Flame of the forest)   3   4   2

Answers at the end

31. Healthy Gujia Recipe

Let's make this delicious Holi snack!

Ingredients
¾ cup wheat flour
¼ cup all purpose flour
2 tbsp Ghee (clarified butter)
1 cup desiccated coconut
1 tbsp chopped cashews
1 tbsp raisins
½ cup sugar
1 tsp cardamom powder

Let's do it!

- ❑ Knead flour, water, ghee and a pinch of salt to make dough. It should be soft. Set aside for 20 minutes.
- ❑ Dry roast coconut, cashews & raisins for a few minutes.

- Add sugar & cardamom powder to the coconut mixture. Let it cool.
- Now take the dough and make 2 inch balls out of it and flatten them to a circle.
- Place the coconut mix in the middle of it.

 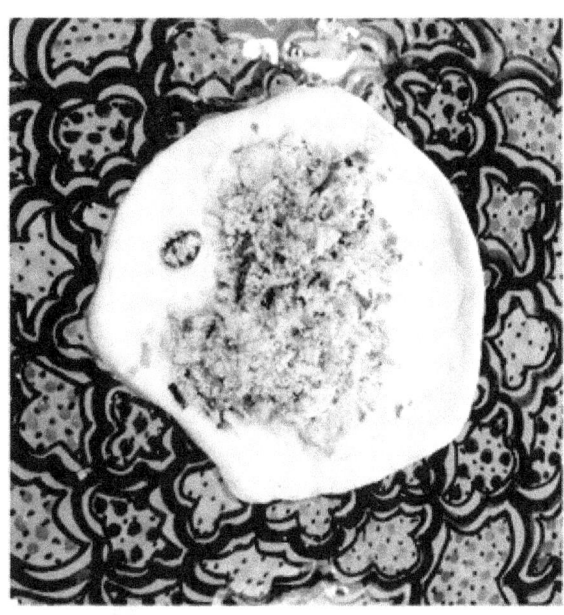

- Close it to form a half moon shape and pinch the edges.
- Place wax paper on baking tray and place the Gujias on it. Bake at 200° for 30 minutes.

32. Fill the Boxes

Fill the boxes with GUL, IA, AND, CHI, HOL, CHK or AHL to reveal the Holi words.

GUJ ☒

PI ☒ ☒ ARI

☒ IKA

TH ☒ ☒ AI

☒ AAL

PR ☒ ☒ AD

☒ NTU

Answers at the end

33. Holi Dance 5 - Madhubala

A Bollywood hit, this song embraces the beautiful folk tunes of Northern India. This choreography is especially suited for ages 3 to 5 years.

FIND IT ON OUR CULTURE CHANNEL
CultureGroove.com/Holi

34. Celebration Tracker

Holi is celebrated on a full moon day. Let's go from new moon to full moon by following this 15-day activity guide.

Day 1	Day 2	Day 3	Day 4	Day 5
Read the Holi book	Solve any of the Holi puzzles	Learn a Holi dance	I am Brave when…	Eat some Gujia

Day 6	Day 7	Day 8	Day 9	Day 10
Help Chintu up the Friendship ladder	Do the flower craft	Sing Finger Family Color Song	Make Pichkari Card	Learn Another Holi dance

Day 11	Day 12	Day 13	Day 14	Day 15
Drink Thandai	Learn about Indian flowers	Do a coloring activity	Make the bonfire lamp	Play Holi

35. Holi Dance 6 – Hindi Finger Family

Sing and dance-along with the finger family and learn colors in Hindi.

Red finger, red finger, where are you?
Here I am, here I am, how do you do?

Laal finger, Laal finger, where are you?
Here I am, here I am, how do you do?

Blue finger, blue finger, where are you?
Here I am, here I am, how do you do?

Neela finger, Neela finger, where are you?
Here I am, here I am, how do you do?

Green finger, green finger, where are you?
Here I am, here I am, how do you do?

Hara finger, Hara finger, where are you?
Here I am, here I am, how do you do?

Yellow finger, yellow finger, where are you?
Here I am, here I am, how do you do?

Peela finger, Peela finger, where are you?
Here I am, here I am, how do you do?

Pink finger, pink finger, where are you?
Here I am, here I am, how do you do?

Gulabi finger, Gulabi finger, where are you?
Here I am, here I am, how do you do?

FIND IT ON OUR CULTURE STATION
CultureGroove.com/Holi

36. Match the Hindi Colors

After singing along with Hindi Finger Family song, match the colors in English and Hindi

GREEN  LAAL

YELLOW  NEELA

PINK  HARA

RED  PEELA

BLUE  GULABI

37. Yummy Moon Phases

Holi is celebrated on a full moon day. Learn about Moon phases with some yummy treats!

Materials: Paper plate, White cream sandwich cookies

Steps: Remove the top layer of the cookie. Cut the cream by different amounts to represent the phases of the moon. Place them on a paper plate and draw an earth in the center using crayons.

38. Spot the 8 Differences

Answers at the end

39. Holi Double Puzzle

Unscramble the Holi words. Next, copy the letters from the numbered boxes to reveal the final message at the bottom.

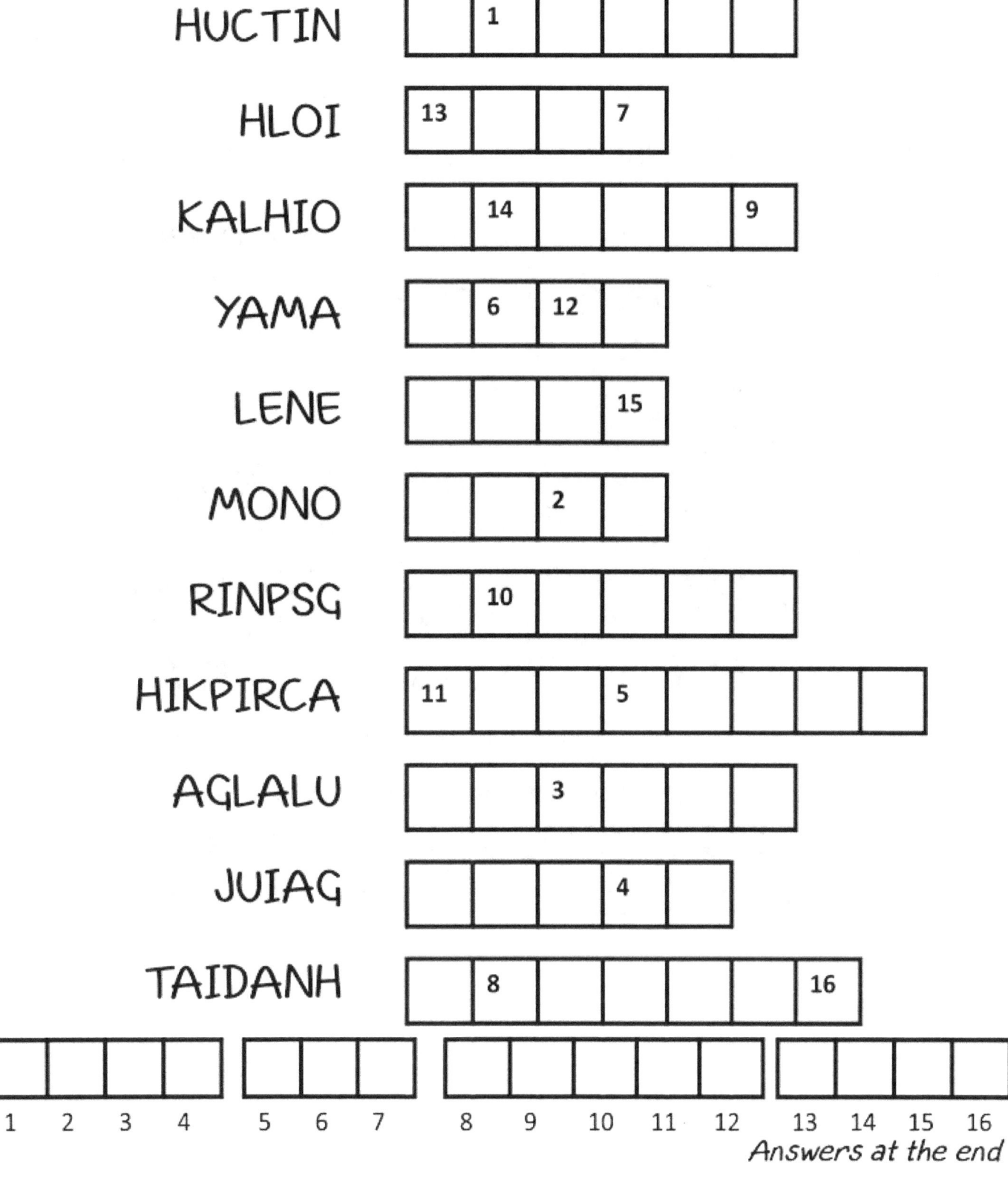

Answers at the end

40. Holi Dance 7 – Jai Jai Shiv Shankar

A modern day remix of a timeless classic, this song is the perfect upbeat way to capture the spirit of Holi. This choreography is best suited for ages 11 and up.

FIND IT ON OUR CULTURE CHANNEL
CultureGroove.com/Holi

41. How many Pichkaris can you find?

Answer at the end

42. Make Holi Colors
Make fun & edible Holi colors at home!

- ☐ Use beetroot to get a vibrant **red**. Simply boil and cool it and use the water for your Pichkari or any water gun.

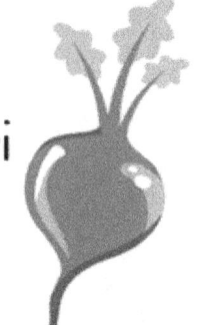

- ☐ Dry mint leaves and crush into a smooth powder. Enjoy some natural **green** Gulaal!

- ☐ Mix turmeric and chick pea flour for some **yellow** color. This paste is also great for your skin!

- ☐ This one makes for a fun project with kids! Mix a cup of corn starch or flour with ½ cup of water and food coloring. Knead it into a dough and let it dry for a few days. Note: you can also flatten the mix to let it dry faster. Crumble it into a smooth powder and get ready to play Holi!

43. Holi Secret Message

Discover the secret Holi message by using the decoding key from below

य ओ उ   अ र ि   ब र अ व ि   अ न द

अ   ग र ि अ त   फ र अि ि न द

DECODING KEY

A	B	C	D	E	F	G	H	I	J
अ	ब	स	द	ि	फ	ग	ह	अि	ज

K	L	M	N	O	P	Q	R	S	T
क	ल	म	न	ओ	प	क्य	र	श	त

U	V	W	X	Y	Z
उ	व	त्र	क्ष	य	ध

Answers at the end

44. Who likes which flower?

Answers at the end

45. Connect the Dots

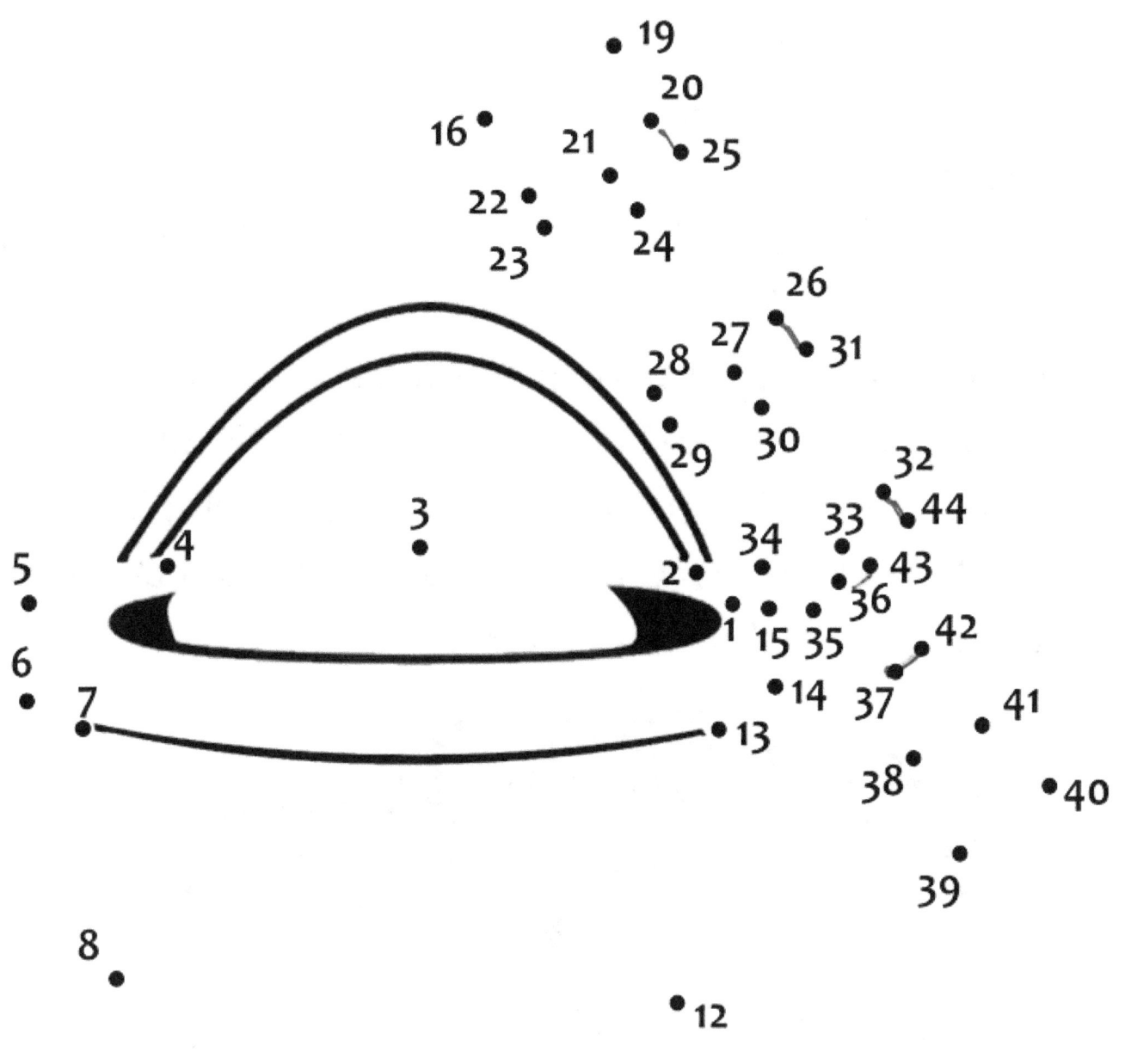

46. Hindi Color Hop

- From CultureGroove.com/Holi download the colored template of the picture on the right.
- Cut out the squares and place them on the floor exactly as shown.
- Starting from the bottom, ask your child to step and hop through the game.
- Every time they step or place their hand on a colored shape, they have to call out the color in Hindi.
- You can make the path longer by using multiple sets of prints. Make it more fun by asking them to complete the course faster and faster!

Hindi Color Hop Contd.

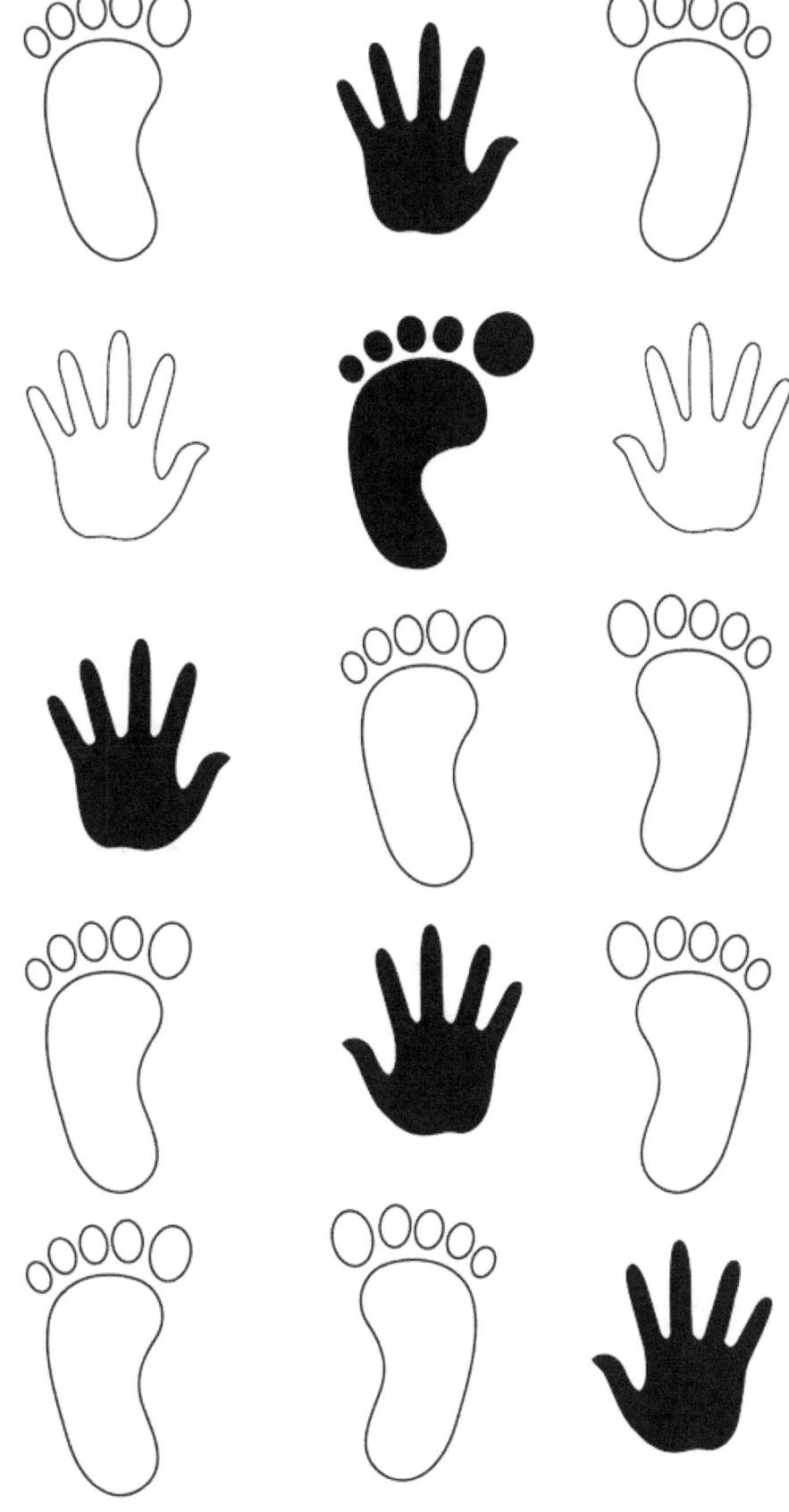

47. My Holi Journal

How did you celebrate? Feel free to decorate with stickers and drawings.

I made...
_____
_____
_____
_____

I read/watched...
_____
_____
_____
_____

This page is intentionally left blank

This page is intentionally left blank

48. Holi Jigsaw Puzzle

Cut the image along the dotted lines. Jumble the pieces. Have fun putting the picture together!

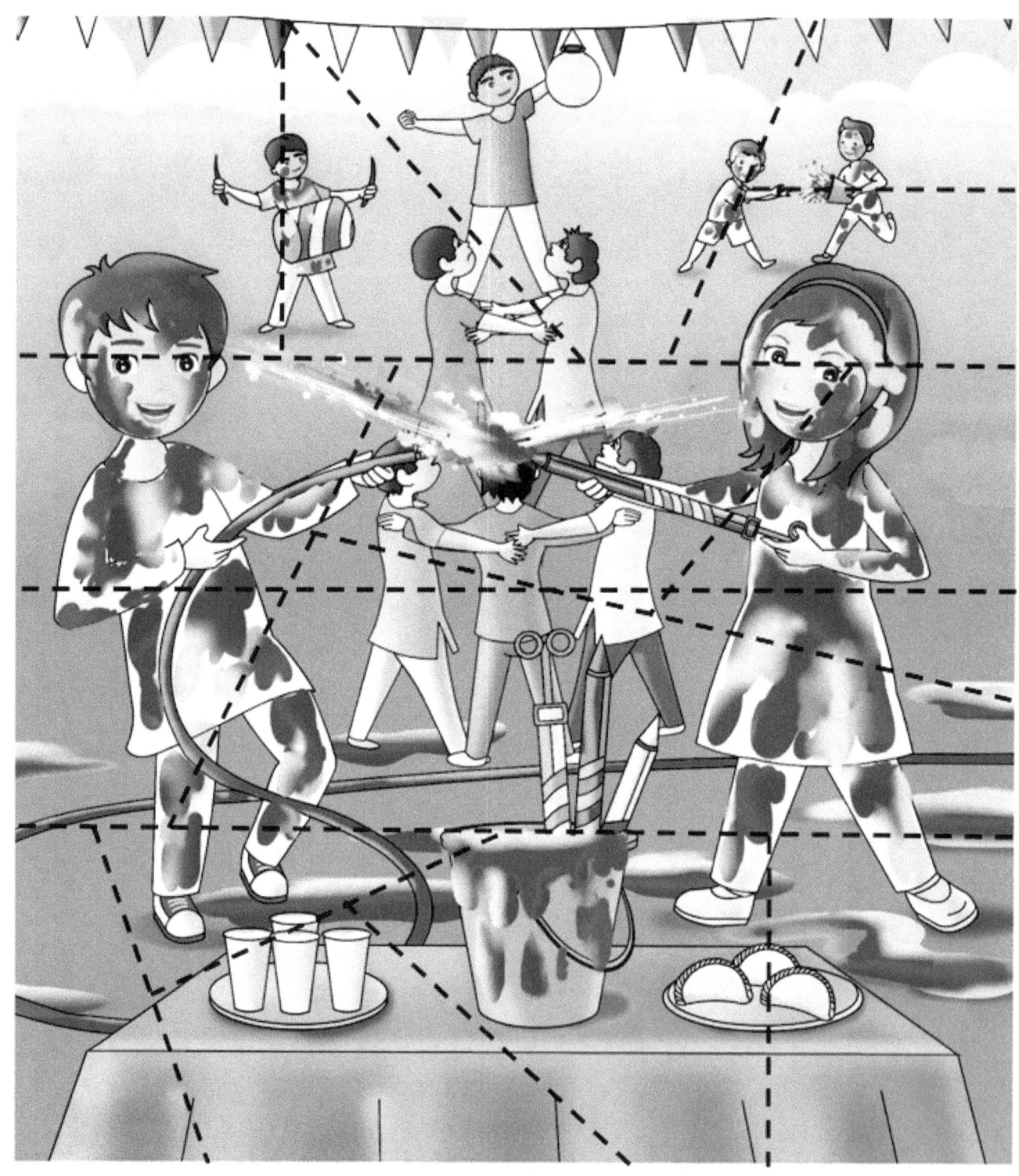

This page is intentionally left blank

49. Prahlad Bonfire Craft

Let's make this glowing bonfire to celebrate Prahlad's victory over Holika!

Materials:
Yellow and orange tissue papers, a transparent plastic cup, brown cardboard piece, LED tea light, popsicle stick.

Steps:
- Cut out Prahad's shape on the left. Color Prahlad.
- Glue Prahlad to the top of a popsicle stick.
- Put the cup upside down and make a small slit in it.
- Slide the popsicle stick in until it looks like Prahlad is standing on top of the cup.

- Cut squares about an inch wide from the tissue papers.
- Scrunch up the tissue papers by pressing them into a ball and then opening them up.
- Stick them all around the plastic cup to represent fire.

- Cut strips of cardboard to make it look like logs
- Place the cardboard strips under the cup.
- Now place an LED tea light inside the cup and place it in a dark spot.
- Enjoy your glow-in-the-dark Prahlad bonfire!

This page is intentionally left blank

This page is intentionally left blank

50. Moon Countdown

Holi is celebrated on a full moon day. Let's do a countdown from half moon to full moon using Moon phases!

☐ Cut the circle below. Stick it on a piece of cardboard. We will call this the moon circle.

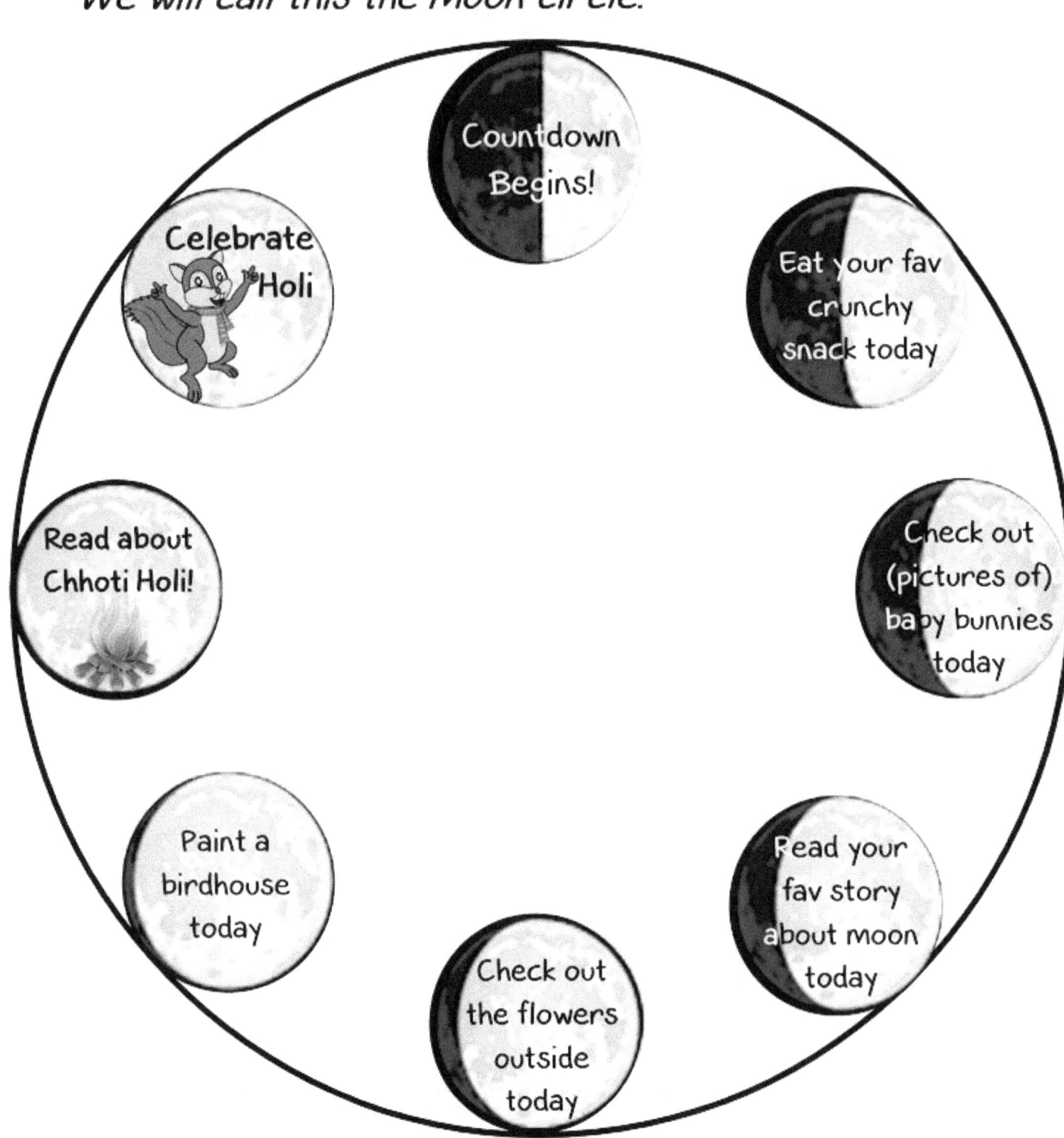

- ❑ Cut another circle of exactly the same size and cut one hole in it, which is the same size as the moon. We will call this circle the cover.
- ❑ Place the cover on top of the moon circle.
- ❑ Using a pushpin, connect the cover to the moon circle. Place an eraser on the back so that the pushpin doesn't stick out.
- ❑ Start your countdown eight days before Holi. Start on T-8 and rotate the circle one day at a time to reveal a new day.
- ❑ Do the suggested spring-time activity and enjoy!

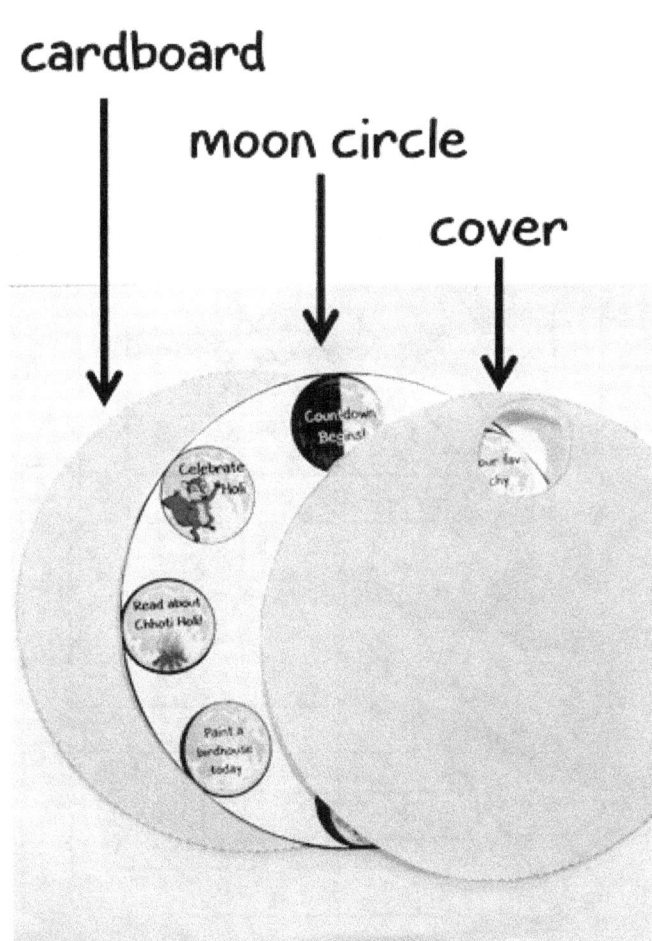

cardboard

moon circle

cover

Answer Key

4. Find the missing letters

<u>K</u>ing, <u>S</u>cared, <u>B</u>oy, <u>M</u>agical, <u>F</u>ire, <u>S</u>it, <u>D</u>isappeared

9. Neel's Holi Crossword

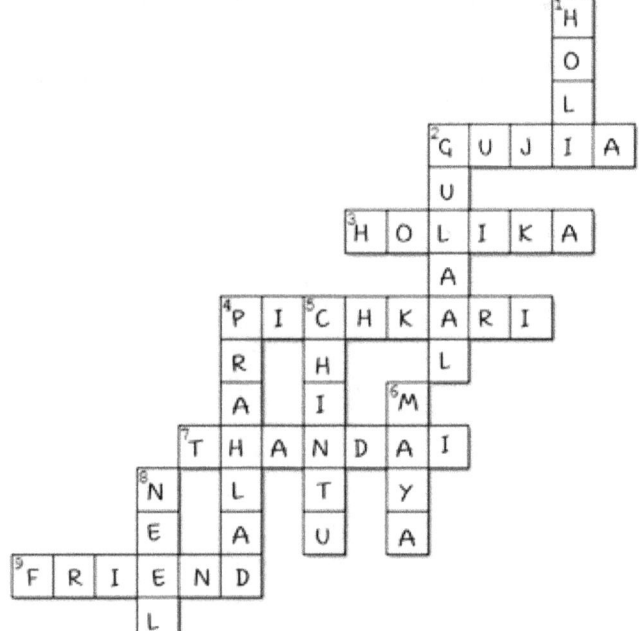

11. Holi Riddles

- ☐ Gulaal
- ☐ Gujia
- ☐ Pichkari
- ☐ Prahlad

21. Find Holi Items

22. Maya's Word Search

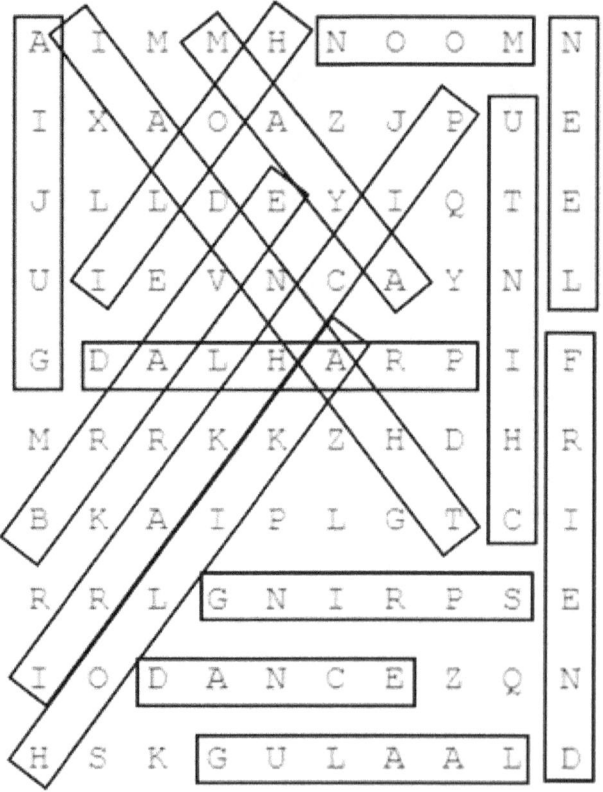

24. Spot & Color
- ☐ Full
- ☐ spring
- ☐ Pichkari
- ☐ Gulaal
- ☐ Gujia
- ☐ Thandai

30. Count the Indian flowers
4, 6, 7, 3

32. Fill the boxes
GUJ<u>IA</u>
PI<u>CH</u>KARI
<u>HO</u>LIKA
THA<u>ND</u>AI
<u>G</u>ULAAL
PRAHLAD
<u>CH</u>INTU

39. Holi Double Puzzle

C	H	I	N	T	U
H	O	L	I
H	O	L	I	K	A
M	A	Y	A
N	E	E	L
M	O	O	N
S	P	R	I	N	G
P	I	C	H	K	A	R	I
G	U	L	A	A	L
G	U	J	I	A
T	H	A	N	D	A	I

| H | O | L | I | | H | A | I | | H | A | P | P | Y | | H | O | L | I |
| 1 | 2 | 3 | 4 | | 5 | 6 | 7 | | 8 | 9 | 10 | 11 | 12 | | 13 | 14 | 15 | 16 |

41. How many Pichkaris can you find?
16

38. Spot the 8 differences

43. Holi Secret Message
You are Brave and a Great Friend

44. Who likes which flower?
Neel – Mogra (Jasmine)
Maya – Gudhal (Hibiscus)
Chintu – Palash (Flame of the Forest)
Ameya – Kamal (Lotus)

About the Authors

Ajanta Chakraborty was born in Bhopal, India, and moved to North America in 2001. She earned an MS in Computer Science from the University of British Columbia and also earned a Senior Diploma in Bharatanatyam, a classical Indian dance, to feed her spirit.

Ajanta quit her corporate consulting job in 2011 and took the plunge to run Bollywood Groove (and also Culture Groove) full-time. The best part of her work day includes grooving with classes of children as they leap and swing and twirl to a Bollywood beat.

Vivek Kumar was born in Mumbai, India, and moved to the US in 1998. Vivek has an MS in Electrical Engineering from The University of Texas, Austin, and an MBA from the Kellogg School of Management, Northwestern University.

Vivek has a very serious day job in management consulting. But he'd love to spend his days leaping and swinging, too.

We have been featured on:

  FOX   ELLE   nielsen

We are independent authors who want to help raise multicultural kids! We rely on your support to sustain our work. Please help:

✓ Drop us an Amazon review at: **CultureGroove.com/books**

✓ Give our books as **gifts, party favors** (bulk order discounts)

✓ Schedule our unique **'Dancing Bookworms'** author visit

Many thanks!